I0766911

# Adulthood of Mystery: A Cultured Peace State of Mind

# ADULTHOOD OF MYSTERY: A CULTURED PEACE STATE OF MIND

Adulthood of Mystery Presents: A Cultured Peace State of Mind

PHEBE ISRAEL

Cultured Peace Services LLC

Charlotte, NC

# Contents

Part II. Visualz

# Dedication

Dear Friends

Thank you for supporting my art movement. By publishing this piece of art it has granted me a platform to speak to you. Energy is never destroyed or created but transferred through forms. On every level I encourage you to transform your energy. By meeting me and allowing me to touch your soul I am forever grateful. When I say I love you , I am just simply saying I value your existence. Cheers to healing and dealing with the past to understand the future.

I Love You,

Phebe Israel

# CulturedPeace

Culture / kəlCHər/ the characteristic features of everyday existence (such as diversions or a way of life) shared by people in a place or time

Cultured / kəlCHərd/ produced under artificial conditions

Peace/pēs/ a state of tranquility or quiet: 2: freedom from disquieting or oppressive thoughts or emotions 3: harmony in personal relations

To gain a culture of peace is to sacrifice everything one holds dear to see your 'neighbor' succeed. The Bible KJVA says in Ecclesiasticus 13:15,"Every beast loveth his like, and every man loveth his neighbor." You must be the passport to create the aura. The living idea of being the change needed to ride the wave. Applying the difference in your daily transactions. Through all the adversity remember to pray. In theory, it is a lifestyle of decisions that may require you to always find a transparent solution to life's everyday problems.

Simply, transform the social atmosphere and make it better. Be the vibe it can never be duplicated; and if you know that jive then, is that hep cat n' canary in the groove. Try to keep it uncomplicated and just ask yourself, why not make someone's day when you have the power to do so? That is a question that I habitually challenge. Find the light if you choose to shine. For Proverbs 4:18 says,"But the path of the just is as the shining light, that shineth more and more unto the perfect day." Mind you, this is not a peaceful process at all. It will require a different type of strength to conquer having an abundant life, by obtaining A Cultured Peace State of Mind.

Boom, picture this if we go back to the survival mode of the fortitude of the fittest and all those mixed conceptualizations taught here in America. There is a time in some of our lives where we have that 'ah-ha' moment! When we realize we are responsible not only for self but for something much more, others. We each have the power and responsibility to untangle the lies of our lives deeper than one can imagine. Reference Revelation 3:9,2:9 KJVA. Then think well, someone has to be a dignified person. Affirm that YOU can be a person of wisdom and knowledge needed to complete the vibe!

In good fashion, most strive to acquire some level of success. Regardless of the resources, it takes an altruistic person to have the ambition to seek some type of change. Hope for our communities and peace for our streets to actually enjoy the culture we create.

Then one day, we are not blind anymore and can discern accordingly. We have started to relearn ourselves and examine everything we thought we knew on a deeper level. In some sense if we are souls with bodies, I wonder if we can tap into a specific frequency within? Can our memory travel through our spiritual souls? We know slavery was and is a very real curse for some, blessing for other's. In 1Kings 8:46 KJVA it states "If they sin against thee, (for there is no man that sinneth not,) and thou be angry with them, and deliver them to the enemy, so that they carry them away captives unto the land of the enemy, far or near;". This did occur but it did not happen to 'all' nations of people. I can say did happen to so-called American Blacks. Thank the Most High God, my bloodline survived!

However, it does raise some serious issues and concerns that not everyone will understand. The bible was weaponized as an attempt to erase our heritage and we are still the 'salt of the earth' today. As Jeremiah 29:7

KJVA states "And seek the peace of the city whither I have caused you to be carried away captives, and pray unto the Lord for it: for in the peace thereof shall ye have peace".

I realized that I will have to endure through the pain for my nation to gain; basically, that is what this book will explain. They^ (society) always say things like, "you are the author of your own story," but we know it's not quite that easy, nor should we expect it to be.

These are poems inspired by oppression experienced over the years in search of spiritual growth that is deeply correlated to the hidden truths of the world.

Maybe this will inspire YOU; my friend, to cultivate your vibe peacefully, even when it rains.


Enjoy the Beautiful Journey

# PART I

# MAIN SQUEEZE

# 1.

# Adulthood of Mystery

Sometimes I feel that I look unfamiliar, just staring in the mirror

It all looks so strange, my body and face, all look the same

Maybe it's the pain

I recognize this feeling of confusion

Last time I felt this urge I thought I was healing

Is that you?

I beg and wonder

I am definitely lost

A tree without roots, these branches are lims

A vine with no stems, your vineyard bears spoiled grapes

Embeded within the forbidden fruit, we are totally sauced^

'Real recognize real' than this is absolutely a delusion

'Real eyes realize real lies', right?

I ran to you the last time

Remember surprise and delight?

Now I am wheeling and dealing, just trying to fight this fright

This baggage is heavy, my legs are shaky

I do not feel strong enough to carry the whole load

It brings me to my knees and ravishes me with stead

I recognize this feeling I have been here before but looks unfamiliar

Adulthood is mysterious and Life is much more

I am searching for the beam because my balance is off

Only truth will satisfy this void

Confess your lies before my father returns to set this jawn^ off

When mushrooms clouds fly the righteous will stand by and watch all wicked die

Adulthood is mysterious and Life is much more

One can never really be sure when to explore what's behind life's mystery door

Jawn/jōn/ person, place or thing

Sauced/Sis-aw-Sed/extremely intoxicated

2.

# Know, No Betta

Little black girl don't you know, no betta

Hiding all that beautiful hair under that name-brand sweater

Dying your crown with the oppressors' ways

Little black boy don't you know, no good

Got the block by the glock, all misunderstood

Missing your knowledge will have you in a maze

Hanging around with your head to the ground

Wishing you could do better if you had better

Realizing you just lacking all the cheddar

Little poor kid, don't you know, no good

Got the entire hood wishing they could

Knee deep in dem' streets appealing to all the creeps

Little feeble girl, don't you know, no betta

No one is home to tell you to lock up that box and act better

Strutting across like a gentle fox, foul play can set this block off like Fort Knox

Don't fall for giving out your snapper for some hep cat who plays like he's dapper

Emotional despair if he would only care or if he would call

Instead, he is at the mall trying to ball, on the game, doing nothing at all

Make them all fallback and close down that sack

Little Hebrew girl, don't you know it's all a show, they domineer you

So you don't know how much you can truly glow

Glowing is growing and growing is changing

Don't you know no better this curse gets worse when you don't find your treasure

Free Jewelry

- *One per crew it matters who you screw*

- The truth is always the truth no matter who tells the lie

- The soul of a man is in his eyes, look deep inside at times they lie

- If you plant a rotten seed, your plant will bear rotten fruit


Hep cat /ha-EP K-at/a guy in the know with all the answers

Free Jewelry / informing one up on 'game'

# 3.

# Twhattt?

What do you love about that pink lady?

Do you love the color that only GOD could choose handpicked especially for you?

How about when she sits up just right?

Do you love how she looks after a clean wax or fresh trim?

Do you love being odorless and disease-free?

Do you love all the strength behind that lock and door?

The keyhole to life but, he prefers the backdoor

How about the way she can spit out a 10-pound baby and still tightly grip a stick?

I love the fact that she can do all that and cum

Twhat^ do you love about your box?

I CUNT hear you

Twhatt did you say?

Is it the Depth or the Power?

Have a great day




Twat/T(h)wät/ A woman vagina; A great word to shout

# 4.

# Disc Jockey

If I was him

Would you agree

You would never say those things to me

Acting like these gems are free

It is damn near a part of me

I make this world spin

I assemble this vibe, don't take me wrong

You tighten up my list and keep matters in check

With no you, there is no me

Wouldn't you agree

The minutiae of things I don't think enough about

How all that piles up

I could really use it if you this take it out and clean that up

What, you don't give a fuck?

You acting like these things are free

I need you to take care of me

I thought last night a DJ saved my life

I can not resist your sensational vibe

I really need you to get this joint jump'n

Please don't take it wrong when I say

Be my slave. Dote after me

That is just what I need to feel blessed today

# 5.

# Mentee

You once untwisted a wrapper

With no intentions on buying the bag

You left one-piece open

Exposed to the elements, my facade inherently changed

Still the same sweet piece but now sticky and soft

Magnetic in nature, lint and fuzz find a new host

Abominably dirty, not even holy water can clean

Unwrap my confectionery love and can enjoy this sweetmeat

Donde' Esta' Papi

Eat Me Now! I am the same piece you abandoned

What I see is what you get

You sold me a dream and I broke the bank to buy

My zeal was golden and my actions were solid

Look deep between the lines there is plenty of space

I became an image and you wanted to gain

I've changed in form, swilled with no flavor

Take a Sip!

In a sense, this is what you transformed

Wishing this consumer had a sell-by dated

A warning label at least I would have survived the storm

Instead, I followed your fallacious thumbs

Your three cups of tea now a icebox in my chest where
my heart used to be

Devour Me Now or Leave Me Be

Fallacious/fə lāSHəs/a mistaken belief

Mentee/men tē/a person seeks counselor

# 6.

# Junkie

Who says junkies only use DOPE

Nope

It all depends on what's dope

I am an emotional hoarder, that hits harder than hope

That feeling I get when I am in the sky

All these things around me and I don't know why

Wishing I could fly and just stay high

Swimming forever in your power over me

Chasing the wave it's not a way to behave

I can only hope you've caught this wave, and rode it before it finds you on the bathroom floor

Talking about how you can not take it anymore

I can help you out and point toward the door

I am afraid that love doesn't live here anymore

Scared of losing you, something I never considered of before

Opened to opportunity, the unity between you and thee

It's a chore nowadays, it's much worse than before

It's mandatory, reclaiming all of your glory

The smile is gone when you are dead inside

Suicide seems like it would be better than hunting a ghost, maintaining any type of high

This is the kind of demon that keeps score

Today, I decided to die

To kill the part of me that needs you so diligently

Burying our treasures deep down in your grave

This freedom I found I don't know how to react

I turned in this key and I Do Not want it back

Afterbirth matters, I needed time to grow

You can no longer use junkie when calling my name!

I am who I am, including not the same

Use my new name when speaking to me, Mane!

I just needed to let all that junk go

I am that I am! Thank GOD I overcame!


Mane/mān/Alternate pronounciation of Man. Head or thoughts.

# 7.

# Poor Me, Pour Me

Poor me

I used to be broken

Now I am just numbing the pain

Paying for all my hearts decisions how could I be so dumb

I'm looking through the looking glass in a brand new way

Indulging in this liquid has gotten me encouraged

I should have never be this parched, thirsty is no way to live

This cup is fearless because I thought I took a loss

Pour Me up and roll the skunk!

If only I would have been braver instead of sauced^

Braver to encounter the days while I was dazed

Strong drink for my sorrows

More L's for tomorrow

I am sure I will fill this later

No hope for the waiter

Poor me and take a pill

I no longer feel sorry, I'm numb

He held my hand with no play in mind

I have shuffled the cards that the dealer dealt

But I do throw in my hand and keep my poker face?

Damn, I answered the call that should have been blocked

Caught up in feelings my trigger is pulled

My mouth is an emotional fool

Let me fill you up

Ooops party foul!! I spilled the cup

Its now a pool of my feelings to clean up

Poor Me, Pour Me

I almost felt sorry for myself...But

I was just drunk

# 8.

# Pool Party

Looking for the answer, its right here. You have to have something, just to be clear

Some call it a kickback or a flow in the beat

when you arrive with your hands are empty, how can that be?

Your entire space, I wish I could erase, even just renovate you

Looks so captivating but it feels so empty

A disgrace with no base

Who created these wounds?

It's hard to recoup with no coupe

Root less making you ruthless with no remorse, of course

I am the fool with no pull, to bring you back in to make you feel full

Splish, Splash, Clap, Bang!

Where is every soul you sold in this game?

I am the one who deserves the name, the fame

I stood up when nobody else came

And look who ended up with all the pain, and shame

This lacuna is desolate with a huge mass in the middle

People stand around naked and afraid to dive in, to explore something a little more

Surviving the crowd where no one is allowed

Screaming and shouting but not saying it proud

It's open but closed, seducing but deserted

The zone is here but the vibe is sold separately!

The prize is a pool party where no one swims but everyone is dressed, or not

Audit your crew effectively, appearances can sometimes get beside thee reflect on the deck timely

27

A CULTURED PEACE STATE OF MIND

Audit your crew effectively, appearances can sometimes get beside thee reflect on the deck timely

# 9

# Green-House Effect

I am consumed in what I used to know

Not realizing that green grows and plants die

Each season has a different effect

At no time does it rain the same

I forgot to change your pot out

Maybe the soil is the same?

I never planted a new seed

Why are these petals are strange?

I do not recognize that flower

When the sun came out how come it gave you no power?

Am I confused? Did I not give you enough room?

Is that not what you needed?

So, I collected my memories and painted a new picture

Can one discern its own nature?

This once seed is now a plant much stronger than before

The flowers sat on display in a store for all to adore

It grew, lived and then; it died.

The spirits whispered through the providence

I have traveled my passage to explore more

Where the sun's rays were strong and the breeze was free

Savor my love and do not pout

I just needed to be placed out

It was the direct light that affected me

The Green-House effect wasn't the best for me

Providence / prävədəns/the protective care of God or of nature as a spiritual power

# 10.

# Mistakes My Mother
# Never Made

It's hard to live up to her

I have made mistakes she had not

As I sat in the late twenties, one kid, married knot

I  perched and reflected, what could it be?

I neglected me, how could I not see

All this time I was tending to someone but not she

Mistakes my mother never made was that she would never forsake thee

She proved to invest the best in me even when I live recklessly

Afraid to dream and live the unknown to take chances on homegrown

I seamlessly recycled a series of illusions with no solutions

Lots of lost love in this world found in a boy with a girl that reflection turned her world

That sheds everyday love and gets in the way love

That no glove love that makes you want to stay love

It's hard to live up to her

She made mistakes I had not

# 11.

# Toxic Strand on My Other Hand

My other hand bears a toxic strand

That intoxicating toxin

That got you acting out of pocket kind of toxic

Your heart keeps me addicted

Your pain pushes me away

Your words spoil in my ears and vanish with my tears

I wondered if I watered your roots would your flower bloom or should I stay away

I tried to hold your stem but your thorns you made me bleed

Infatuated with your plant, your seed, the soil

Joy, pain, sorrow, at times I don't want a tomorrow

That chronic kind of toxic I am addicted to your pain

Beguiled with your drip I am not able to drive

My eyes swollen shut because of the hive

I hijacked your honey and your nectar is sensational

Enmeshed in your populace, enthralled in your embrace

Possibly with no prophecy, for all cinch is gone

Hoodwinked

Nothing can grow here, it is clear as mud, translucent

You gave up the ghost so I can no longer entertain the host

My other hand has a toxic strand I just can not stand


Hoodwinked    /ho͞od͵wiNGk/deceived    by    false appearance

Translucent    /tranz lo͞osnt/clear from    disguise    or falseness

# 12.

# Cyclone

You behave like a treacherous storm

Dangerous cycles with uncertain winds

Blowing through everything

You are changing directions fast

I can not see your eyes with your murky past

Words act as your disguise

Listening to you I've been binded to this size

My heart wants to believe this is a test, mindful unfair trial

I can hardly tell you anything as you kick through the door, acting impossible to adore

I am pleading with you to calm down

Now I am gone in the wind without bounds

I needed you to protect me from the rain, I wanted you to heal my pain

I stood outside waiting for you and a cold is all I gained

Weakened by the weekends you when kept my indoors

It led me to a breakdown and it changed my core

I am someone that I no longer recognize

Your demons blew right through this place

Our foundation was faulty it is all superficial

Debris so thick, Ground zero

So much trauma not even a therapist can mend

No support group

Not even a retail-rama deal can contend

Your unstable emotions devastated my world

The results from your actions there is nothing left

Let me read this bible in a new light, historical will

Off to rebuilding, it's only up from here

My spirit survived your cyclone this time, just to be clear

Next time, I know now to call on Yah the Most High Lord of Host

He will send his angel's to throw down against your demons to protect the ghost

# 13.

# Breach Of Trust

The bond is broken, you just lied

I am bewildered and lost

My faith in this belief system paid the ultimate cost

All praises to the Most High God of Israel

The light covered the entire fee

I was so consumed until he got involved with me

Now I'm in the spirit and you are in the clear... Dark

Damn bruh, you always had somebody in the ear

Spitting that shit that nobody asked to hear, I mean dumb bodies

I am not as timid as I was before to walk right out this door

I almost took your words for golden, that is on me... light

That time you were lying saying everything will be alright

It is ironic how the truth shines through

I will love you always and this truly hurts

Weirdly enough it all seems to work

This is my wake up call ere to my relapse

If I continue this descend I will never reign again

I'm so thankful that the truth has prevailed

I can not give up in this spiritual fight

Only sooth matters after tonight


Sooth/sooTH/truth

# 14.

# Mourning After

The morning after hours are the worst

There is no plan b for this course

I mourn for what I lost

Grief is all I gained

You chose someone else and I can not get you of out my system

Saying your name, I can not be tamed

This break hurts

There is no way I can not wrap it but there is no bandage sufficient to entrap it

In the morning after I rose without you

This feels like an enigma, how could I ever have doubted

I obligated you here, it was so clear

I am the mourning after; your ambiguous disaster; the not-so-perfect storm

The trails chiseled can not be recovered

I am so luxated the path is gone

My footed sole is heavy, no fugazy

I needed you here it was so clear

The Morning after sol is hazy

There is no pill to release this fiery

To hold this pain of how I feel

Oh My God please can I heal me?

I call your name but your response is not the same

It hurts so much my heart is in pain

My dear, can you hear? Do you even care?

I am still standing around, just waiting

Is it not clear?

I am mourning after your sol left here


Luxated / ləksāt-id/to throw out of place

Fugazy / Foo-gazie/ in the sense of "fake"

# 15.

# Blow through me

Take a deep breath

Hold it and release it softly

That same breath you are letting go

Belongs with the ocean just so you know

The waves seem so brave hitting the wall

Flow-through me moreover after I fall

My justified body is here, what is the matter

I am after your soul, your pith is the goal

Your flesh is burdensome, guilt weighing you down

Surround me; make me feel found

Breathing deeply to center thee

The she who menstruates my mind, I'm too blinded to see

Your spirit is within my heart, where it's between my ears

Your frequency is all around, I can sense you near

Calm me with your presence, silence me with your words

Your Law is My Heritage and teaches me your ways

I am committed to the commandments

I am no longer led astray

The only way is to Read, Pray and Apply before I die


Pith/the essence of something

# 16.

# Happiness is Relative

Sometimes it rains, at times it doesn't

When I get my feet wet it makes me want to hop, skip and flop

When I laugh to heal from crying there is no way I can be stopped

Do not let this frown keep you from coming around

Do not leave me down here when I want to come up

I am in a state of being a proportion of something else

This is not my situation I accepted the circumstances

My current space is selective at most

I am in control but I am not the host

Sometimes I am here, at times I am there

As long as I am not stuck, I do not have a care

Embrace being that stylish mole, the sugar on the grits, the avocado to the toast, and the icing on the cake!

It makes no sense to chase what I can provide and what they can  not take

My happiness is mine! Whether I weather the storm, or not

It is all relative! It is whatever, you choose, or not

Happiness/hap-E-nis/ state of being happy

Relative/rel-auh-tiv/ in proportion to something else

# 17.

# Repent

Those who are wise understand love is not free

This agreement to learn is a decree

More real than any deal ever sealed

These laws were left for us to live by

These commandments are put in place to help us survive

Read it in-depth, way past the lies

Coming up in this world I learned how to;

Tend to a friend

Staying afloat on a boat with holes

Fire with no coals

Trying to sing no song with a dance

We know how that goes, blind leading the blinded

Everybody hopes but nobody knows

Don't get scared of a letdown

If your faith is in man that is all that's around

My lips are unclean, my words come out mean

My demeanor is meek

I gave it all up to fix my crown

I repent lo, I have done this all wrong

Life without 'bread' is like an unsolved equation

I submit to the truth no matter the situation


Repent/rə pent/ to turn from sin and dedicate oneself to the amendment of one's life

# 18.

# Freedom is
# Expensive

Priceless they say

All-day everyday

We Fight, We Pray

We would love to solve the world's problems

And lay in the grass n' play

Stay all day but it will be expensive

What's Freedom to You?

I'll wait but bossing up will be extensive

Selection is success

Separation is key

We can never take a loss or the enemy will gain

With her head at the guillotine

Tie your rights to a yoke of iron

Possession of the con called pipeline potential

Toss you in a cage and make you understand why the bird sang

Entrenched in the investment, there's no way I am clocking out

I'm humming a new tune

Freedom has to be mental! This is spiritual warfare!

It feels like a sin not being able to be present and win

But the truth will set us free!

How do we find it?

Do we know it when we see it?

Faith walk they call it, it is something for sure

Quarantined in this shell we are meant to endure

There is no going outside at your own will, not even to

the hair store, only to get pills, meals, and service on your automobiles

Did you get permission?

Where is your slip, a hall pass, if you will. What is the deal?

Freedom is expensive the cost is relative at most

Would you be willing to give up the ghost?

To lose everything, even the host...

Land of the free but my ancestors paid

They don't even have respect to maintain their graves

There is a highway over them and a schoolhouse beside

The blood, sweat, and tears they try to deny

The price tag is large but the payment is minimum

He hung us from a tree and sodomized thee

Then he dared to say "Not Me" ...

Elongating our bodies they made us learn how to deal

Did you climb up there? Was it worth that fight?

They said it was a choice. Do you see it that way?

The only lashes whipped now are the ones that she is batting

She's no angel with wings, do not be blinded by the bling

Sweet chariots will deliver us to the home if we are ready, when they swing low enough with the messiah

The ticket is the covenant and the price tag are the commandments

Guaranteed to will cover the entire cost; a worldly sacrifice sho' Nuff' the fee

The law of your heritage was once hidden and can now be regained

It takes reading for Israel to maintain their glory

No matter how they try to conceal the truth

The bible will always be the final root

Precept by precept, line by line

There is a lot of explaining to do with this timeline

Why did this happen and how could this be?

I never returned to the place from where they stole me

Freedom / frē-duhm/personal liberation as opposed to bondage or slavery

Quarantine / kwȯr-ən-ˌtēn/a restraint upon activities or communication of persons or the transport of goods designed to prevent the spread, of disease or pests; a period of 40 days

# 19.

# Ah Ha

Enlightenment of inspirational verbiage.

- It takes more than one person to create a body. 'Double single'
- The greatest opposition may be internal. Do not get tunnel vision
- People are nefarious by fault. It's better to be altruistic
- 'The world' thinks she got away with slavery.  It Will Not!
- Seek repentance over acceptance. 'Be connected within'
- The bible is so creepy because it's TRUE. Songs of Solomon 1:5 KJVA
- Being a good parent is time-consuming. 'Reap what ye sow'
- There is beauty in sacrifices. 'Endure to the

Core'

- There can't be 2 heads and no tail and vise versa. 'Humility is key'
- Organized non-white groups scare society's power position. 'Scare them anyways'
- Understanding who we are individually is a secure feeling. 'Seek deep and pray'
- Faith and fear cannot share the same space. 'Meditate to navigate '
- Your current situation is not permanent but it can feel like it. 'Keep pushing, it worth it'
- Stop sharing pivotal moments with non-believing souls. 'Save time and energy'
- Carrying the weight for bad decisions is so heavy. 'Seek Counsel'
- They do hide things in books. Propaganda is a real tactic. Turn off the TELEVISION
- There is always a "clean up woman" somewhere waiting on things to fall apart
- What is meant for you will always be for you no matter the hate. 'Acquired Taste at best'
- Why not make someone's day when you can. Simple kind acts of humanity keep the world alive.
- Parenting has changed and so has the world. 'Societal Inflation'
- Mating is a dance and it's harder for those with no rhythm. 'Prove thy friend'

- Love is something that is taught it does not come naturally.'Be self-aware'
- Correction is caring. Silence is not. Not everyone is mature enough for reconstruction. 'Know your audience'

# 20.

# BlackMail

They^ tried to ruin us, they though they could

Their intentions were vile, and meant no good

They^ broke 'em down and turned 'em out

A bill held over the head of the house

They say "let 'em live and let 'em work" she thought she could cover the fee unknowing of the costs

Not quite mature enough to add

Not wise enough to understand the total score

No one can make a man, he decides that himself

I trusted the product that went stale on the shelf

Is it worth my mentality because my vibe is off?

They kidnapped my king and returned a thug, a nigga, a sloth

Psychosis is the result of all the illusions

No, PTSD does not qualify as a diagnosis

Post Traumatic Slave Syndrome^ is what that is known as

They busted my buck and tried to erase my past

A social experiment with nowhere to grow

Was I supposed to fix this mans' soul?

The content is too deep to unfold

There's nothing more felicific than a sealed letter

Saturated and dazed, incarcerated for days

Once I opened you up your color was bleak

The ransom note had our family at sake

They held a new price over my seed to stunt the glow

My black male is and was as good as gold

Return to the sender!

The ransom was way too high and would pull us low-low

We were blackmailed it damn 'sho ain't no joke, yo

59

Felicific  /fe·li·cif·ic/fee-luh–sif-ik/promoting  increased happiness.

*"Post Traumatic Slave Syndrome"/ defines as the residual impacts of generations of slavery and opens up the discussion of how the black community can use the strengths we have gained in the past to heal in the present – Dr. Joy DeGruy*

They ^ /the Powers that be; Society, 'The Man'

# 21.

# Onyx Seethe

I am black rage!

She committed a crime and served no jail-time

It makes my blood boil just thinking about it

If I act on it I will sow turmoil

'It is' what they warn y'all 'bout!

If I greenlight it, nothing will sprout

Your agnostic voice has approached me to the edge

Lost for hope as I stare at the ledge

When I decide to scream n' shout and act all angry, how y'all been making me out

I'm out of pocket, now? How?

Amidst thyself you sparked a nerve, even shocked myself. I should have curved

I showed you what you were warned about

Hey, no fair you took me there!

Am I supposed to be held to a different tier, that we were unaware of?

My rights were removed and I am encaged

There is no way we are on the same page

Racial assassination with no hesitation

They will pick up a phone to call their pal to destroy our nations at the touch of a dial

Be cool, they say, I am all chilled out

Place us behind bars without rehabilitation. Experimental disrespect!

Repossessing our history ensuring the endurance misappropriation

Causing our community to bethink themselve and forget our nations

Mental health is a real complication

Not understanding your roots will rotten your nations' fruits

Anxiety with no sobriety

No sane can toke away cognitive dissonance

Valley of the dead, we just need our souls to rise through the bones

Congregating is the goal, we need order in our lives

It helps to talk about what lies deeper than blood diamonds

Even when we raise ourselves the pain is generational

It's overly sensational

It is Onyx Seethe


Bethink/bih-th-ink /to consider; recall

Seethe/ sēth/to suffer violent internal excitement

# PART II

# VISUALZ

Photography By:

Deangelo 'Bossdogg' Crawford of BosslandFilmz

Antonio B of A+Media

Brandon Withers, My homie 'Chilly' nephew

Make-Up By:

Darell Wilson

Styled By:

Phebe Israel

CULTURE

# Jargon

Bethink /bih-th-ink /to consider; recall

Culture / kəlCHər/ the characteristic features of everyday existence (such as diversions or a way of life) shared by people in a place or time

Cultured / kəlCHərd/ produced under artificial conditions

Fallacious /fə lāSHəs/a mistaken belief

Felicific /fe·li·cif·ic/fee-luh-sif-ik/promoting increased happiness

Free Jewelry / informing one up on 'game'

Freedom/ frē-duhm/personal libertation as opposed to bondage or slavery

Happiness/hap-E-nis/ state of being happy

Hep cat /ha-EP K-at/a guy in the know with all the answers

Hoodwinked / hŏŏd wiNGk/deceived by false appearance

Jawn /jōn/ person, place or thing

Luxated / ləksāt-id/to throw out of place

Mane /mān/Alternate pronounciation of Man: 2: Head or thoughts

Mentee /men tē/a person seeks counselor

Peace /pēs/ a state of tranquility or quiet: 2: freedom from disquieting or oppressive thoughts or emotions 3: harmony in personal relations

Pith/the essence of something

Post Traumatic Slave Syndrome/the residual impacts of generations of slavery and opens up the discussion of how the black community can use the strengths we have gained in the past to heal in the present – Dr. Joy DeGruy

Providence / prävədəns/the protective care of God or of nature as a spiritual power

Relative /rel-auh-tiv/ in proportion to something else

Repent /rə pent/ to turn from sin and dedicate oneself to the amendment of one's life

Sauced /Sis-aw-Sed/ extremely intoxicated

Seethe / sēth/ to suffer violent internal excitement

Sooth /sooTH/ truth

Twat /T(h)wät/ A woman vagina; A great word to shout

Translucent /tranz loōsnt/ clear from disguise or falseness

# Sources and Resources

Sources

The Holy Bible/1611 KJV-Apocrypha

Post Traumatic Slave Syndrome by Dr. Joy De Gruy

Resources

www.merriam-webster.com/dictionary

www.urbandictionary.com

www.dictionary.com

www.thesaurus.com

# Phebe's Final Thoughts

*E*verything *ain't for everyone and that is quite alright. What is meant for you is already yours and once you accept it, you will receive the ultimate gift. The present.*

Want to tell me how you inspire to cultivate the vibe?

Share Your Thoughts on Social Media.

www.ingramcontent.com/pod-product-compliance
Lightning Source LLC
Chambersburg PA
CBHW051123300726
48981CB00022B/522/J